# Praise for
## *The Sex Lives of College Students*

In *The Sex Lives of College Students*, Dr. Sandy Caron provides an important glimpse into the sexual lives and attitudes of college students, both today and as compared with 30 years ago. Her analysis is spot on, as she reflects on findings in light of children and youth being raised in a society that is both sex saturated and sex silent.

We "don't talk about it" at home, school, house of worship, or in the doctor's office. So young people are guided by sexually explicit media, i.e. pornography, as the education about what sex looks like. More students are faking orgasms, nearly all, like the porn stars, shave all their pubic hair, and the double standard still lives on. At the same time, today's students are more tolerant, e.g. of LGBTQ friends, and women can have "friends with benefits," thus having casual sex in ways men have historically done.

Of particular note for this sexual scholar trained by the late Dr. Sol Gordon, who championed parents as the first and in many ways more important sex educators of their children, 53% had asked their mother a question or two, while 75% had never asked their father any questions about sex.

We can do better to prepare young people for their adult lives as sexual beings. Dr. Caron's highly accessible "viewbook" tells us what is, which may well help with needed education about sexual health, relationships, and pleasure.

— **Betsy Crane, Ph.D.**
Retired Professor, Center for Human Sexuality Studies, Widener University

How do college students experience and express their sexualities? Has this changed over time? Here we find painless statistics, no boring numbers! New generations of college students, seeking to personally solve the mysteries of sex and sexuality, will find their answers here in a colorful, compelling, easy-to-comprehend format. Their parents will be interested, too. As a sexuality researcher myself, I have great appreciation for the information Dr. Sandy Caron has compiled and how she has presented it.

— **Carol Rinkleib Ellison, Ph.D.**
AASECT certified sexuality educator and therapist,
and author of *Women's Sexualities. Generations of Women Share Intimate Secrets of Sexual Self Acceptance*

# Praise for *The Sex Lives of College Students*

In an age when rampant misinformation about sex permeates the airwaves, television screens, and movie houses of America, Sandy Caron pulls us back into reality-- one filled not with pompous sexual 'achievement,' but with sexual insecurities, gender inequities, contradiction, paradox, and clear places to celebrate and to worry, especially for supposed advances in women's sexual liberation. An enjoyable, accessible read that will delight anyone wanting a clear look at undergraduate sexuality across time."

— **Breanne Fahs, Ph.D.**
Associate Professor of Women and Gender Studies at Arizona State University
Author of *Performing Sex and The Moral Panics of Sexuality*

*The Sex Lives of College Students* provides a snapshot of young adult sexual behavior over the past 30 years as well as an analysis of trends over that same time period. The outstanding graphic design of the book makes for very easy information processing. It is a quick read, yet provides a great deal of useful, scientifically-based information in a more comprehensive way than many longer and more detailed resources on sexual behavior and attitudes.

— **Terri D. Fisher, Ph.D.**
Professor Emeritus of Psychology, The Ohio State University
Teaching Professor of Psychology, Director of the Office of Undergraduate Research and Scholarship, The University of the South

It is my pleasure to recommend Professor Sandra Caron's book *The Sex Lives of College Students,* now in its third edition. Since it was first released, this book has made significant contributions to our knowledge and understanding of human sexuality, especially at that typically highly charged and often confusing time of life: the college years. The book is grounded in solid scientific research and written in an informative and entertaining style. This third edition expands on the first two editions, further enlightening us about college students' sexual behaviors, thoughts, and emotions that are not frequently discussed openly. As was clear from the first two editions, Dr. Caron's contributions to this field will have a lasting influence and is a must read for students, professors, parents, and anyone who desires a greater understanding of these topics. I highly recommend it.

— **Roger R. Hock, Ph.D.**
Professor of Psychology Emeritus, Mendocino College
Author of *Human Sexuality, 4th Edition; Forty Studies that Changed Psychology, 8th Edition; It's My Life Now: Starting Over After an Abusive Relationship, 3rd Edition* (with Meg Kennedy Dugan); and *Psychology, 2nd Edition* (digital text with Dr. Amy Marin)

# Praise for *The Sex Lives of College Students*

For decades, we've been stuck with fact-free magazine polls, misguided myths, non-representative psychology studies, and just plain wild guesses about what college students actually do sexually. Now we finally know, thanks to years of hard work by Dr. Sandra Caron. Based on reliable data from thousands of students, her new book *The Sex Lives of College Students* tells us what they do, what they think they do, why they think they do it, and how they like it. This is a funny, serious, insightful, surprising, and ultimately reassuring book. It's easy to read, hard to put down, and a wonderful conversation-starter between mates, parents and adolescents, or people just starting a relationship. I've admired Sandy's teaching for years. Now I admire her writing as well.

— **Marty Klein, Ph.D.**
Sex therapist and author of *Sexual Intelligence: What We Really Want From Sex, and How to Get It* (HarperCollins)

Undergraduates who take the human sexuality course want to know what their peers are doing. Dr. Caron provides the data in her *Sex Lives of College Students*. The book is focused on the questions students want answered, is beautifully illustrated and presented in an outstanding format — the question, the percent(s), and the change across time — all at a glance. A no nonsense revelation of the sex content students are interested in, this book gives meaning to the "science" in "Family Science."

— **David Knox, Ph.D.**
Professor of Sociology, East Carolina University
Co-author with Susan Milstein, *Human Sexuality: Making Informed Decisions* (BVT, 2021)

Has anything related to sex behavior changed in the past 30 years? The quick answer most would give is "of course"! How do we know? And has it changed in a sexually healthy way? *The Sex Lives of College Students* provides a unique look over time of what many of us wonder, given the media presentation of values and images. 'Sex Lives' is a HUGE "gold mine" in a very small package. Wonderful visuals, and presentation of data. Yes… "data" that is fun to read and can be used with adults and youth alike to stimulate important conversations.

— **Konstance McCaffree, Ph.D., CSE, CFLE**
Past President AASECT (American Association of Sexuality Educators, Counselors & Therapists) AASECT Certified Sexuality Educator
Sexuality Consultant, Adjunct Professor Widener University

# Praise for *The Sex Lives of College Students*

*The Sex Lives of College Students* is a sexual health bible. Imagine having a window with a view of the sexual attitudes and behavior of nearly 7,000 students. Some of the most unspoken sexual health issues are presented clearly for all to see and process. If our goal is to have young people understand their own sexuality and make healthy sexual decisions this is a must read for high school and college students and their parents.

**— Mark Schoen, Ph.D.**
Founder, SexSmartFilms.com
Producer, Transthemovie.com

• • • • • • • • • • • • • • • • • • • • • • • • • • • • • • • • • • • • • • • • • • •

*The Sex Lives of College Students* is a uniquely impressive and intriguing bird's eye view into the world of young people. Dr. Caron's findings – gathered from more than 30 years of research – will not only inform the work of college professors teaching human sexuality, but also serves as a blueprint for secondary education teachers and public health policy makers as they prepare their teaching priorities; as well as parents, as they prepare the conversations that are necessary and relevant.

**Bill Taverner, MA, CSE**
Chief Editor, *American Journal of Sexuality Education*
Founder, Sex Ed Lecture Series

• • • • • • • • • • • • • • • • • • • • • • • • • • • • • • • • • • • • • • • • • • •

Third
Edition

# THE SEX LIVES OF COLLEGE STUDENTS:

### Three decades of attitudes and behaviors

# Sandra Caron, Ph.D.

## Foreword by Dr. Clive Davis

## Illustrated by Val Ireland

# Acknowledgement

Some of my best teachers have been my students. I want to thank all the college students who took the time to respond to the human sexuality survey in order to provide us with greater insight and understanding.

**Designed by Val Ireland**

**Printed in the United States of America**

**ISBN-13: 978-0-9912601-7-1**
**Maine College Press, Inc**
**P.O. Box 351**
**Orono, ME 04473**

**SexLivesofCollegeStudents.com**

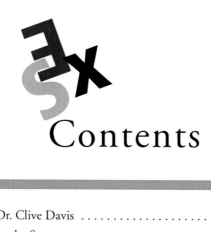

# Contents

Foreword by Dr. Clive Davis . . . . . . . . . . . . . . . . . . . . . . . . . . . . . . .iv

Introduction to the Survey . . . . . . . . . . . . . . . . . . . . . . . . . . . . . . vii

## Thirty-Year Data Set

**Sexual Behaviors**

Ever done it? . . . . . . . . . . . . . . . . . . . . . . . . . . . . . . . . . . . . . . . . . 2

When was your first time? . . . . . . . . . . . . . . . . . . . . . . . . . . . . . . . 4

Do you use protection? . . . . . . . . . . . . . . . . . . . . . . . . . . . . . . . . 6

Birth control of choice? . . . . . . . . . . . . . . . . . . . . . . . . . . . . . . . 8

How many people have you been with? . . . . . . . . . . . . . . . . . . . . .10

How do you feel about the number of people you've been with? . . . . . .12

Ever lied about how many people you've been with? . . . . . . . . . . . . . .14

Ever faked it? . . . . . . . . . . . . . . . . . . . . . . . . . . . . . . . . . . . . . . . .16

Ever masturbated? . . . . . . . . . . . . . . . . . . . . . . . . . . . . . . . . . . . .18

How old were you when you started masturbating? . . . . . . . . . . . . . .20

How often do you masturbate? . . . . . . . . . . . . . . . . . . . . . . . . . . . .22

Ever had sexual experiences with someone of the same sex? . . . . . . . . .24

**Sexual Attitudes**

Abstinence until marriage? Say what? . . . . . . . . . . . . . . . . . . . . . . . .28

Is virginity important to anyone anymore? . . . . . . . . . . . . . . . . . . . .30

Do you like oral sex? . . . . . . . . . . . . . . . . . . . . . . . . . . . . . . . . . . . . .32

Thoughts about anal sex? . . . . . . . . . . . . . . . . . . . . . . . . . . . . . . . . .34

What's love got to do with it? . . . . . . . . . . . . . . . . . . . . . . . . . . . . . .36

How comfortable are you having a gay friend? . . . . . . . . . . . . . . . . .38

What are your feelings about abortion? . . . . . . . . . . . . . . . . . . . . . .40

**Parental Influence**

What would mom say if she knew? . . . . . . . . . . . . . . . . . . . . . . . . . .44

What would dad say if he knew? . . . . . . . . . . . . . . . . . . . . . . . . . . . .46

Ever asked mom a question about sex?. . . . . . . . . . . . . . . . . . . . . . .48

Ever asked dad a question about sex? . . . . . . . . . . . . . . . . . . . . . . . .50

Did your parents influence your views on sex? . . . . . . . . . . . . . . . . .52

**Safer Sex and HIV/AIDS**

How concerned are you about HIV? . . . . . . . . . . . . . . . . . . . . . . . . .56

Has your behavior changed in response to HIV? . . . . . . . . . . . . . . . .58

How likely are you to:

    - ask how many sex partners the person has had? . . . . . . . . . . . . . . .60

    - try to guess if a partner might be HIV+ . . . . . . . . . . . . . . . . . . . .62

    - take fewer precautions if a partner doesn't seem like type . . . . . . . .64

    - ask for a monogamous relationship? . . . . . . . . . . . . . . . . . . . . . . .66

    - ask a partner if she/he has been tested for HIV? . . . . . . . . . . . . . .68

    - have both of you tested for HIV? . . . . . . . . . . . . . . . . . . . . . . . . .70

    - discuss using a condom before sex? . . . . . . . . . . . . . . . . . . . . . . . .72

    - refuse sex without a condom? . . . . . . . . . . . . . . . . . . . . . . . . . . . .74

**Difficult Side of Sexuality**

Do you know anyone who has had an STI? . . . . . . . . . . . . . . . . . . . .78

Ever had an STI? . . . . . . . . . . . . . . . . . . . . . . . . . . . . . . . . . . . . . . .80

Know anyone who has had an abortion?. . . . . . . . . . . . . . . . . . . . . .82

Ever been involved in a pregnancy that ended in abortion?. . . . . . . . .84

Do you know anyone who has been raped?. . . . . . . . . . . . . . . . . . . .86

Have you ever been raped? . . . . . . . . . . . . . . . . . . . . . . . . . . . . . . . .88

Ever had an involuntary sexual experience? . . . . . . . . . . . . . . . . . . .90

Were you sexually abused as a child? . . . . . . . . . . . . . . . . . . . . . . . . .92

## Newer Data Set

Have you ever used the morning-after pill? . . . . . . . . . . . . . . . . . . . . .96
Do you do a monthly self-exam? . . . . . . . . . . . . . . . . . . . . . . . . . .97
Penis size? Breast size?. . . . . . . . . . . . . . . . . . . . . . . . . . . . . . . . . .98
Have you ever shaved? . . . . . . . . . . . . . . . . . . . . . . . . . . . . . . . . . .99
Sex without a condom? . . . . . . . . . . . . . . . . . . . . . . . . . . . . . . . . .100
What have you done sexually? . . . . . . . . . . . . . . . . . . . . . . . . . . . .102
Technology and sex . . . . . . . . . . . . . . . . . . . . . . . . . . . . . . . . . . .104
Planes, trains and automobiles . . . . . . . . . . . . . . . . . . . . . . . . . . .106
Ever lied to get someone in bed? . . . . . . . . . . . . . . . . . . . . . . . . . .108
Ever gotten someone drunk? . . . . . . . . . . . . . . . . . . . . . . . . . . . .109
Had an intentional one-night stand? . . . . . . . . . . . . . . . . . . . . . . .110
Ever cheated on a partner? . . . . . . . . . . . . . . . . . . . . . . . . . . . . . .111
Why are you most likely to have sex? . . . . . . . . . . . . . . . . . . . . . . .112
How does your sex life stack up? . . . . . . . . . . . . . . . . . . . . . . . . . .113
Longest you've gone without sex? . . . . . . . . . . . . . . . . . . . . . . . . .114
Greatest age difference? . . . . . . . . . . . . . . . . . . . . . . . . . . . . . . . .115
The adjective that best describes sex? . . . . . . . . . . . . . . . . . . . . . .116
Favorite position? . . . . . . . . . . . . . . . . . . . . . . . . . . . . . . . . . . . .117
How often do you reach orgasm? . . . . . . . . . . . . . . . . . . . . . . . . .118
Are you satisfied? . . . . . . . . . . . . . . . . . . . . . . . . . . . . . . . . . . . . .119

**Conclusion** . . . . . . . . . . . . . . . . . . . . . . . . . . . . . . . . . . . . . . . .121
**About the Author** . . . . . . . . . . . . . . . . . . . . . . . . . . . . . . . . . . .127
**Contributors** . . . . . . . . . . . . . . . . . . . . . . . . . . . . . . . . . . . . . .129

# Foreword

by Clive M. Davis, Ph.D.

Emeritus Associate Professor of Psychology, Syracuse University
Past President of the Society for the Scientific Study of Sexuality
Past President of the Foundation for the Scientific Study of Sexuality
Former Editor of *The Journal of Sex Research*

I met Dr. Sandra (Sandy) Caron nearly 40 years ago when she came to my office at Syracuse University to introduce herself. She told me about her work as an undergraduate at the University of Maine and her plans to pursue a doctoral program at Syracuse University. Over the course of our conversation, we discovered that we shared a scientific interest in understanding the sexual attitudes and behaviors of our countrymen and women, and in sharing that knowledge with our students through formal coursework and peer educational programs. We also learned that we were both "Mainers," having grown up in towns only a few miles from one another (although our "growing up" was a generation or so apart). Thus, we found we "spoke the same language" in more ways than one. And we Mainers can be different! Since that first meeting, I have learned much more about Sandy, and we have shared much together, ultimately becoming colleagues and friends. I am honored and pleased to be able to say a word to two about Sandy and this book, *The Sex Lives of College Students*.

No one has collected comparable data over such a long time span. As you will see, these "snapshots" are often fascinating, especially if we look at them in relation to other trends in our culture over this same period of time.

First, the book. The contents derive from more than 30 years of data obtained from an annual survey of college students enrolled in Sandy's basic human sexuality course at the University of Maine. The study is unique. Nearly 7,000 students have answered the survey questions. Thus, the results offer considerable insight into the attitudes and behaviors of a diverse group of young adults, at specific points in time — and over time. Although the data are not longitudinal in the statistical sense (i.e., comparing the same people over time), the similarities and the differences between and among the groups over the years are instructive, suggesting changes that may have occurred over time.

No one has collected comparable data over such a long time span. As you will see, these "snapshots" are often fascinating, especially if we look at them in relation to other trends in our culture over this same period of time. Are the results representative of our society at large? Again, we cannot be sure, but they are certainly suggestive, given the consistencies in the data. The results are also valuable in another way: For the students who provided the answers to questions about their beliefs, attitudes and behavior, the results offered them a perspective, helping them understand their own sexualities in the context of their generation. In addition, they — and we who are the readers of this book — can gain insight into the sexualities of those students, as well as our own.

Sandy Caron is also unique. All of us are, of course, but some of us are more unique than others. The mere fact that Sandy had the foresight to collect — systematically — this large body of data over this lengthy period of time is remarkable. Many of us who have taught large human sexuality courses have used surveys of our students' beliefs, attitudes and behaviors, but few of us have had the foresight, the determination and the persistence to do so systematically over 30 years. Furthermore, almost no one has compiled and analyzed his or her data in such a way that the findings contribute to our knowledge about similarities and differences between groups of people (e.g., men compared to women) — and over time. Perhaps the most important characteristic of Sandy's personality is her enthusiasm. She is a great teacher because she is involved and committed, and convinces students that they, too, can be invested in learning about themselves and others. She makes learning fun. Enjoy her, as I have, through her work.

— Clive M. Davis, Ph.D.

# Introduction

**What do nearly 7,000 college students have to say about sex?**

**What do they do?**

**What do they think?**

**How do they feel about it?**

**How has the media and Internet influenced their actions?**

**Compared to 30 years ago, is sex really different today?**

In this third edition of *The Sex Lives of College Students* results are presented of a human sexuality survey administered over the past three decades (from 1990–2020) to thousands of college students ages 18–80. Responses by 6,654 college students between the ages of 18–22 are compiled here. Many of the questions originated from a survey administered in the 1970s and 1980s by the world-renowned sexuality educator, Dr. Sol Gordon at Syracuse University. As my mentor and advisor for my doctoral degree in human sexuality, Dr. Gordon encouraged me to continue to distribute the survey in my own human sexuality classes when I became a faculty member at the University of Maine.

The more than 100-question survey has been administered during the first week of every human sexuality class at the University of Maine since 1990. The undergraduate class has a capacity enrollment of 350 students and regular waiting lists. In 2010, several new questions were added and refined to address the latest issues and trends, including the use of social media to facilitate relationships and use of morning-after pills.

## Above all, the findings raise awareness about students' understanding of sex matters

The goal is to survey college students' attitudes and behaviors at the start of the course. And while many of the students enrolled in the human sexuality course are majoring in the social sciences, the students represent every college and major at the university.

Many take the popular class as an elective to "unlearn what they've learned." For all, the academically rigorous class is also a personal journey, helping them learn how to be comfortable talking about sex and their sexuality.

The survey results are shared with the class to demonstrate the value of sex research and to serve as a springboard for discussions. The students are able to compare themselves to other studies of college sexual attitudes and behaviors, as well as to results from previous students completing the survey. Above all, the findings raise awareness about students' understanding of sex matters (e.g., despite an image of college life involving sex every weekend, half the respondents say they have gone a few months without sex) and difficult issues (nearly a third of the students surveyed responded that they have had an involuntary sexual experience, and more than half the students know someone who had been raped).

In many cases, the survey data help students let go of "bedtime fables" — such misconceptions as "bigger is better" and the misconception that everyone knows the secrets to sex. The latter is particularly detrimental when men and women find themselves disappointed in their relationships when their sexual partners fail to satisfy them.

**Among the most telling disparities between perceptions and reality: the question about faking orgasms.** Despite the 1960s Sexual Revolution and what appears to be more openness than ever before concerning relationships, the data found that a quarter of men and two-thirds of women say they have faked orgasms and that number has gone up — not down — over the 30 years. Those numbers tell us that we've lost touch with what sexual relationships are supposed to be about — enjoying ourselves rather than faking pleasure and satisfaction.

Similarly, the lower number of women who said they masturbate (only two-thirds of women compared to nearly 100 percent of men) speaks to the failure to know ourselves and what turns us on. And without that self-knowledge, how can we tell a partner what feels good/what we prefer?

Those survey responses tell us we still have a long way to go before people own their sexuality. The survey reinforces the fact that young adults are generally comfortable pursuing sexual relationships, but often fail to openly discuss sexual issues. What's needed is the confidence of sexual partners to engage in honest conversations about what pleasures them most. Some of the results suggest that the double standard is alive and well when we see that college men are more likely to inflate the number of sex partners they have had, while more women underreport; and college women are much more likely to say love is important in sex, while many men say love is not important at all.

The survey also shows progress in a number of areas, including greater acceptance of sexual diversity and awareness of the importance of safer sex and sexual responsibility, which has resulted in lower numbers of STIs and abortions.

---

**The Sex Lives of College Students** raises awareness, addresses the issues and provides perspective on the trends through the past three decades in the sex lives of college students.

---

In this, the age of the Internet, young adults contend they are informed and free of the guilt and hang ups of their parents' generations, yet most college students have many questions regarding sex. While some know how to proactively get accurate answers to their questions, or had good sex education classes in high school or parents who had open, honest communication about sex, many more college students seem to have a junior high mentality when it comes to sexuality — they may not know much more than what they learned in a middle school class on puberty. With today's technology, there's a sea of accessible half-truths and misinformation about sex. The trick is to find accurate information that heightens awareness, informs decision-making, and promotes healthy lifestyles and well-being.

**The survey data serve as a reality check on the sex lives of college students.** Despite the perception that all college students are regularly hooking up, their survey responses indicate that, overall, they are neither feeling overly liberated sexually nor jumping into bed with multiple partners. Instead, the survey shows a range of opinions and experience in sexual relationships.

College students have lots of questions around sex and, depending on the quality — and sources — of the sex education they received as teens, some may even have some "unlearning" to do. College is such a critical time for young people making decisions about relationships. It is a time of new beginnings, changes and discoveries. It is an opportunity to be informed and be more comfortable with their bodies.

As our future leaders, it's important for them — and those who care about them — to understand and help them "own" their sexuality as part of a healthy lifestyle.

Without information, including the correct information, too many young adults end up having inflated expectations and engaging in sexual acts with little meaning. They wind up thinking that good sex is about how one looks and performs. As reflected in the media, young people live in a sex saturated but sex silent society in which there is not enough informed dialogue.

The hope is that The Sex Lives of College Students can jumpstart the dialogue.

However, this book is not the be-all and end-all survey on the sex lives of college students. It is not representative of a cross-section of all college students across the country, but it does give us a glimpse of a student sample from a mid-size public research university. Indeed, it is a unique perspective informed by a 30-year data set (spanning from 1990–2020), analyzed with the help of University of Maine colleague Dr. Sid Mitchell. The data facilitate the tracking of trends and comparison of changes in attitudes and behaviors.

Because of its longevity, the survey includes not only the views of today's college students, but also those of their parents, including some who may have sat in the same lecture hall taking the course in human sexuality.

I invite you to visit The Sex Lives of College Students website (**sexlivesofcollegestudents.com**) to view the survey, and to post questions and comments to inform the next edition of the book. In addition, you can follow us on Facebook (The Sex Lives of College Students) and Twitter (#sexlivescollege).

## The Demographics
### The sample: 6,654 undergraduates attending the University of Maine

| | |
|---|---|
| Age: | 18–22 years |
| Gender: | Two-thirds women; one-third men |
| Year in College: | From first-year students to seniors |
| Race: | Most White/Non-Hispanic |
| Religion: | More than half Christian |
| Relationships: | Half in a serious relationship |
| Orientation: | Most self-identified as heterosexual |

# Sexual Behavior:

## 1990–2020 Data

1. Ever done it?
2. When was your first time?
3. Do you use protection?
4. Birth control of choice?
5. How many people have you been with?
6. How do you feel about the number of people you've been with?
7. Ever lied about how many people you've been with?
8. Ever faked it?
9. Ever masturbated?
10. How old were you when you started masturbating?
11. How often do you masturbate?
12. Ever had sexual experiences with someone of the same sex?

# Ever done it?

**College men and women were asked, "Have you ever had sexual intercourse?" The overwhelming majority of college students**

# 87% report that they have had sexual intercourse.

**This is not to say there are no college virgins, but certainly there are few.**

There has also been a leveling of the playing field between men and women. Despite the notion that men are more interested and more sexually active than women, there is little difference between college men and women who report having had sex (88% of men and 87% of women).

Free of parental supervision and living in co-ed residence halls with hundreds of students their same age, it is no surprise that the proportion of college students who say they have had sexual intercourse increases by class standing. In other words, the longer they are in college, the more likely they are to experience sexual intercourse. By the time they are seniors 9 out of 10 college men and women have had sex.

## Results over 30 years:

In the past three decades, **not much has changed in terms of the percentage of college students reporting that they have had sexual intercourse.** Despite spending nearly $2 billion to promote abstinence-only-until-marriage "education" since the 1990s, there has been little to no change in college student behavior.

1990s to today

# NO CHANGE

in % of college students having intercourse

**Across all respondents, 87% (n=5,811) indicated they have had sexual intercourse.**

The percentage of those who have had intercourse increased across years in college.

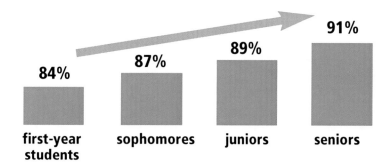

84% first-year students

87% sophomores

89% juniors

91% seniors

# When was your first time?

**College students were asked, "At what age did you first have sexual intercourse?"**

Most college students report that their first experience with sexual intercourse occurred in high school. Of the 5,811 college students who say they have had sex, most (88%) had their first experience by age 18

typically when they were

## 16 – 17 years old

More women say they lost their virginity closer to age 16, while men say their first time was closer to 17.

**High School** 60%

## Results over 30 years:

**Despite the perception that teens are having sex at earlier and earlier ages, the age of first intercourse has remained relatively unchanged in the past 30 years, with most experiencing first intercourse at age 16 or 17.**

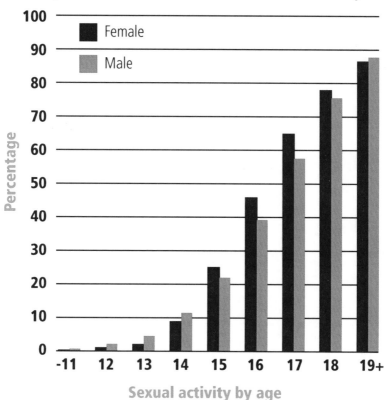

Looking at the percent who say they lost their virginity in their teen years reveals the dramatic increase in sexual activity

# Do you use protection?

**College men and women who have had sexual intercourse were asked, "If you had sexual intercourse during the past three months, did you or your partner use birth control every time?"**

The good news is the majority of the 5,118 students who say they had sex in the last three months

# 81% affirm that they used birth control every time.

**On the down side, this means nearly**

# 1:5 did not

YesYes  YesYes  No Yes  YesYes  Yes No

## Results over 30 years:

The other piece of good news is that over the past 30 years, **there has been an increase in the number of college students who say they use birth control every time.** Reports of birth control use have increased from approximately 75% in the early 1990s to nearly 85% of today's students saying they use it every time.

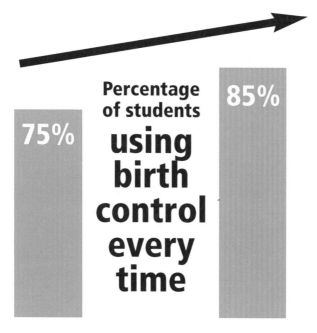

# Birth control of choice?

**Those college men and women who said they had sexual intercourse in the past three months were asked, "What method(s) of birth control did you or your partner use?" (Check all that apply.)**

The most popular methods of birth control used by college students are:

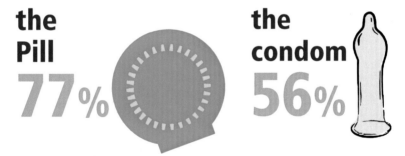

**the
Pill
77%**

**the
condom
56%**

The use of the IUD has increased in the last decade. While almost no one used the IUD in the 1990s and early 2000s, today 15% of college students report using the IUD.

**Other methods,** such as spermicides, diaphragm or fertility awareness, are little used **(10%).**

## Results over 30 years:

It is encouraging to see that the number of **students using the Pill, condoms and IUD increased over the past three decades.** Specifically, Pill use remained high, ranging from 80% in the early 1990s to 75% today. Condom use increased from approximately 45% in the 1990s to about 60% today. IUD use increased from nearly 0% in the early 1990s to 15% today.

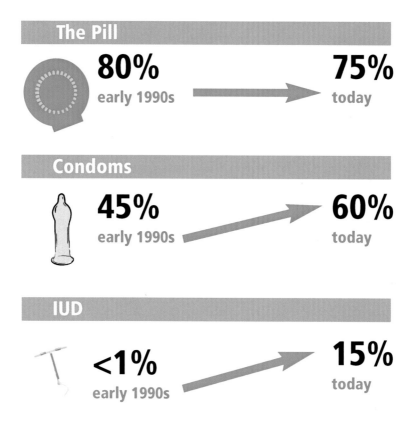

**The Pill**

**80%**
early 1990s

**75%**
today

**Condoms**

**45%**
early 1990s

**60%**
today

**IUD**

**<1%**
early 1990s

**15%**
today

# How many people have you been with?

**Answers ranged from 0–25 or more sexual partners when college men and women were asked, "How many sexual partners have you had in your lifetime?"**

We hear a lot about "hooking up" and "friends with benefits," creating an image of college life involving a different sexual partner every weekend. However, the average number of sex partners for college students is 3 to 4 partners. Yes, a third of college students say they have had five or more partners, but another third have had just 1 or 2 sexual partners.

## the average number
### of sex partners for college students is

# 3 to 4

Few students (11%) indicate that they have never had a sexual partner, while the majority of students (89%) have had at least one.

Upperclass students report more sexual partners than underclass students.

*(Note: "Sexual partners" is not necessarily limited to sexual intercourse.)*

## Results over 30 years:

It may come as a surprise to learn that over the 30-year span of this study, **the incidence of having five or more partners has remained largely unchanged.** That's right. While today's college students may think having multiple partners is unique to their generation with their use of terms like "hooking up" and "friends with benefits," just as many college students 30 years ago were having multiple partners. But back then, it was called "casual sex."

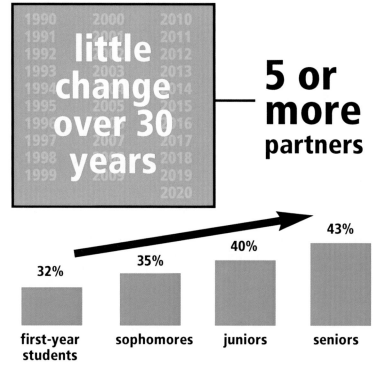

Upperclass students report 5 or more sexual partners than underclass students.

# How do you feel about the number of people you've been with?

**College men and women were asked, "How do you feel about the number of sex partners you have had?"** Students could indicate if they felt they have had more, average or fewer partners than most people.

 **Half of college students think everybody's having more sex than they are**

**— even those who are having the "average" of 3 to 4 partners, as found in this sample.**

So while half (50%) think they have had fewer partners, a small percent (12%) actually feel they have had more partners than most people.

Only about a third (38%) feel they have had an average number of sexual partners. What's interesting to consider is that most of those students (63%) had actually had more than the "3 to 4 partners" average found in this sample — they had 5, 10 or even 20 or more partners. Perhaps this is a way for these students to justify a higher than average number of partners. Or maybe it's because they are in the dark about what their peers are doing, so they are left to guess how they compare to others.

## Results over 30 years:

Looking over the past three decades, it has been more common for students to feel that **all their friends are seeing more action than they are.**

50% think they have had fewer partners, a small percent (12%) actually feel they have had more partners than most people.

# Ever lied about how many people you've been with?

**87% tell the truth**

**College men and women were asked, "If a woman asked you how many sex partners you have had, would you tell her: A number higher than you've really had? A number lower than you've really had? Or the correct number?"** They also were asked how they would respond if a man asked them and if their best friend asked them.

Most of the students (87%) say that they would tell the truth about how many sex partners they have had, no matter who asks them — a woman, a man or their best friend.

However, one in eight (13%) would not tell the correct number (i.e., they would lie).

**Women say less**

**Men say more**

**We see hints of the double standard in those who would lie.** Most women say they'd tell a lower number of sex partners when asked by a man or a woman. Men say they would say a lower number when talking to women, but say a higher number when talking to other men.

On a more concerning note, the more partners a student says they've had, the more likely they say they would lie about it. For example, 76% of college students with five or more partners lied. The take-home message is not to rely on asking someone how many sex partners they have had. You cannot expect an honest answer, especially from those who have had many partners.

## Results over 30 years:

**1990s** **today**

**No change**

Looking across the past three decades, the proportion of **students who lie about the number of sexual partners they had** remains largely the same.

# Ever faked it?

**College men and women who have had sexual intercourse were asked, "Have you ever faked an orgasm?**

## Faking an orgasm is extremely common, especially for women.

Of the 5,811 respondents who say they have had intercourse, more than half (58%) indicated they have faked an orgasm. They say they aren't just doing it — they are performing it. It reflects the difference between what is really happening for them in sex and what they think should be happening.

**Many more college women (70%)** **say they have faked an orgasm.** And while the idea that women fake orgasm may be understandable to some, the idea that men can fake may seem impossible to many.

**However, 28% of college men** **report they have faked an orgasm.**

## Results over 30 years:

Whether to avoid hurting their partners' feelings, build up their partners' egos or reinforce that there is nothing wrong with them, an alarming number of students have turned to faking in the past 30 years.

**40%**  The **Big** **'O'**  **65%**

**1990s**  **vs.**  **today**

**Faking orgasm increased**
from just over a third in the early 1990s
to nearly two-thirds of students today.

**Most of the rise can be attributed to women's behavior.** For college women, faking behavior has increased dramatically over time – from less than half to over three-quarters of college women today saying they have faked an orgasm.

# Ever masturbated?

**College men and women were asked, Have you had ever masturbated?**

Three-quarters (78%) of college students say they have masturbated. Not surprising, most of those who say they masturbate are men.

**Yes**

**78%**

**of all students**

**Of those who have not masturbated, the majority are college women:**

**29% women**

---

**4% men**

In fact, one-third of college women say they have never masturbated as compared to a fraction of college men (29% vs. 4%).

As women progress through college and gain a greater understanding of their body and their sexual response, as well as greater sexual experience, more women report they have masturbated (increasing from 64% of first-year women to 78% of seniors).

## Results over 30 years:

**Looking across the 30 years, there has been an increase in the number of college students who say they have masturbated.** Since most men masturbate, the increase is due to the great numbers of women who say they pleasure themselves — from about 60% in the early 1990s to nearly 75% today.

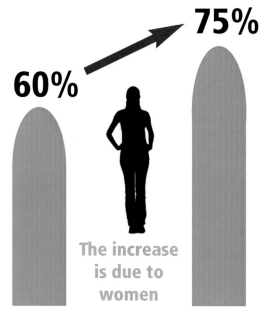

60%

75%

The increase
is due to
women

# 1990s vs. today

Acknowledgement of this increase in women's masturbation can be seen in the popularity of such factors as sex toy parties on college campuses.

# How old were you when you started masturbating?

## College students were asked, How old were you when you started masturbating?

Of the 5,190 respondents who said they masturbate, most college students (79%) say they have masturbated by the age of 16.

## College men and women differ in terms of when they started masturbating. Men indicate a much younger age for first masturbation (average age of 13), while women report a more even distribution for their age of first masturbation (ranging from 11 or younger to 19 and older). Three-quarters of college men (77%) say they started masturbating by the age of 14, while less than half of the college women have (45%).

| Typical age Men | Typical age Women |
|---|---|
| **13** | **11, 12, 13, 14, 15, 16, 17, 18, 19** |

## Results over 30 years:

**Looking across the past three decades, the average age of first masturbation has declined.** However, this trend is attributed to more girls saying they first masturbated in their later teenage years (e.g., 15 to 18 years old); it is not among those who were 14 or younger.

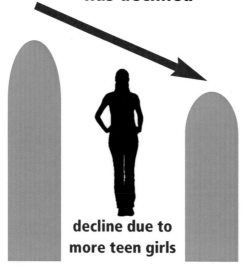

**average age of first masturbation has declined**

**decline due to more teen girls**

**1990s vs. today**

# How often do you masturbate?

**College students were asked, "Do you masturbate now?"** and then asked to indicate how often. Response options ranged from "A few times in my whole life" to "More than once a day."

**College men are much more likely to indicate they masturbate once a week or more compared to college women (72% of men vs. 34% of women).**

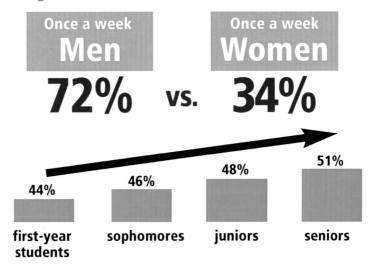

Once a week
**Men**
# 72%

**vs.**

Once a week
**Women**
# 34%

44%
first-year students

46%
sophomores

48%
juniors

51%
seniors

The proportion of college students reporting they masturbate once a week or more increases with class standing.

**Results over 30 years:**

Today, more so than in the past 30 years, there are more college men and women who report masturbating once a week or more—from less than 40% in the early 1990s to more thn 60% today.

There is an increase in masturbation for

## both men & women

since 1990

1990                                today

# Ever had sexual experiences with someone of the same sex?

### Students were asked, "Where do you see yourself along Kinsey's sexual behavior rating scale?"

Options ranged from 0 = Exclusively Heterosexual Experience to 6 = Exclusively Homosexual Experience.

The infamous "Kinsey Scale," developed back in the mid-20th century by pioneer sex researcher Alfred Kinsey, acknowledges that sexual behaviors can range from "0 = Exclusively heterosexual" to "6 = Exclusively homosexual" and offers a way to examine same-sex experiences.

While the majority of college students (80%) consider themselves exclusively heterosexual (0 on the Kinsey Scale), 20% do not.

In fact, women are more likely than men (17% vs. 6%) to say they consider themselves a 1 on the Kinsey Scale, meaning heterosexual with an incidence of same-sex behavior.

**80%**

**Have not had a same-sex experience**

## Results over 30 years:

Looking over the past three decades, **there has been a significant increase** in the number of college students who indicated they are a "1" on the Kinsey Scale (heterosexual with an incidence of same-sex experience). This is especially true for college women. Since the time of the kiss between Madonna and Brittany Spears at the MTV Video Music Awards in 2003, there's been a significant rise in the percentage of women who consider themselves a 1. A significant increase occurred from the early '90s, when only 5% of women identified themselves as heterosexual with a same-sex experience to as high as 25% today saying they have had a same-sex encounter. Whether it is making out with a girlfriend for their boyfriend's pleasure, or simply same-sex experimentation as part of normal sexual development, it is interesting to see that most of these women do not consider themselves bisexual (a 2, 3 or 4 on the Kinsey Scale).

**There's been a significant rise in the percentage of women who consider themselves a '1' on the Kinsey Scale.**

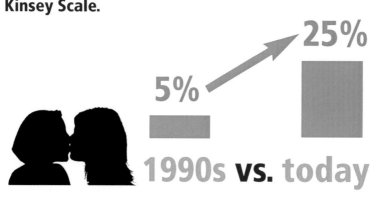

25%

5%

1990s vs. today

# Sexual Attitudes:

## 1990–2020 Data

1. Abstinence until marriage? Say what?

2. Is virginity important to anyone anymore?

3. Do you like oral sex?

4. Thoughts about anal sex?

5. What's love got to do with it?

6. How comfortable are you having a gay friend?

7. What are your feelings about abortion?

# Abstinence until marriage? Say what?

**College men and women were asked their opinion about the acceptability of premarital sex and given three options:**

- "It's all right for everyone, including myself."

- "I'm against it for myself, but what others do is their business."

- "It's morally wrong for everyone."

**93%**
**acceptable for everyone**

**The overwhelming majority of college students (93%) feel premarital sex is acceptable for everyone.**

**5%**
**acceptable for others**

Only a small percentage feel it is not okay for themselves, but acceptable for others (5%), and even fewer (2%) think it is wrong for everyone.

**2%**
**wrong for everyone**

**There was no difference between the acceptance of college men and women on this issue.**

## Results over 25 years:*

College students' acceptance of premarital sex has remained high and unchanged over the past quarter century despite the rise in funding for abstinence-only-until-marriage programs.

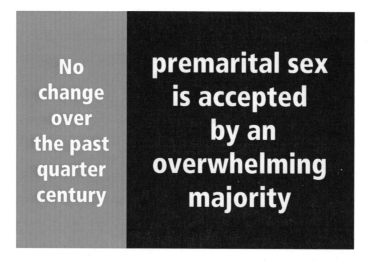

No change over the past quarter century premarital sex is accepted by an overwhelming majority

That is a 180-degree turn from how their grandparents' generation viewed premarital sex.

*Note: This question was dropped from the survey after 2015.*

# Is virginity important to anyone anymore?

**College students were asked about their thoughts on virginity when considering a life partner (both their own and their prospective partner's virginity status) and given several options.**

They were asked to indicate if they were a virgin, and then asked to choose:

"I plan to choose a life partner who is a virgin"

or

"I plan to choose a life partner who is not a virgin,"

or

"Whether my prospective partner is a virgin or not is irrelevant."

## The majority

# 79%

of the college students surveyed felt that whether their partner is a virgin is **irrelevant** when choosing a life partner.

**There was no difference between college men and women** who reported that a prospective partner's virginity is irrelevant (81% vs. 79%).

**However, remnants of the double standard still exist when we look at those who say their partner's virginity status matters.**

More men want a virgin

**If virginity status matters**

More women want a non-virgin

College women (17%) are much more likely than college men (11%) to say they want a sexually experienced (nonvirgin) life partner. Correspondingly, college men (8%) are much more likely than women (4%) to indicate they want a life partner who is a virgin.

## Results over 25 years:*

**Since 1990, there has been a decline in the proportion of college students indicating that virginity is irrelevant in choosing a life partner.** This is primarily due to an increase over the past 25 years in the proportion of women who indicate a preference for a life partner who is not a virgin. More women today say they want their partner to be sexually experienced.

*Note: This question was dropped from the survey after 2015.

# Do you like oral sex?

**College men and women were asked, "What are your personal feelings about oral sex?"** Options ranged from "I think it is totally acceptable" to "I think it is wrong and should be illegal."

**Yes?**  **No?**

**Of the 6,654 college students surveyed, nearly everyone indicated oral sex is** totally acceptable **92%**

Granted, these days, most don't even consider it "real sex."

Nearly every college man (98%) indicated oral sex is totally acceptable, while fewer college women say they feel this way (90%).

The proportion of college students who say they feel oral sex is totally acceptable increased by class standing. In other words, the longer they are in college, the more likely students feel oral sex is totally acceptable — from 91% of first-year students to 95% of seniors.

## Results over 30 years:

**Looking across the 30 years, acceptance of oral sex has remained high,** just as we know from the literature that such behavior has become commonplace over the past few decades.

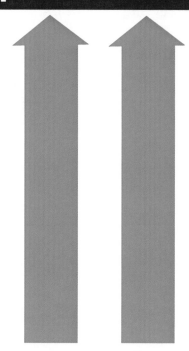

acceptance of oral sex

1990s to today
**remains high**

# Thoughts about anal sex?

**College men and women were asked, "What are your personal feelings about anal sex?"**

## Options ranged from

 **"I think it is totally acceptable." 1/3**

**"It's not for me but what others do is their own business." 1/3**

**to**

**"It is unpleasant, illegal or wrong." 1/3**

Despite all the hype in pornography that portrays anal sex as something that is incredibly popular, only a third (35%) of the college students say anal sex is totally acceptable. Whether it's to please a partner, try something new, avoid pregnancy or maintain one's virginity, few college students rate anal sex as acceptable.

Another one-third (30%) say that while they personally find it unacceptable, what others do is their own business. The final one-third say that they either find the whole idea unpleasant (19%) or feel anal sex is disgusting (15%). Very few feel anal sex is wrong and should be illegal (1%).

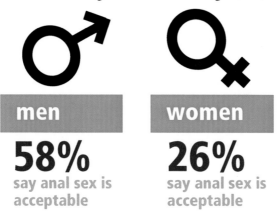

**men**

# 58%
say anal sex is acceptable

**women**

# 26%
say anal sex is acceptable

When comparing their thoughts on anal sex, more than half of college men (58%) feel anal sex is totally acceptable, while only a quarter (26%) of college women feel this way. It is no surprise that so few women rate it high, considering how many women report it is uncomfortable or downright painful.

Upperclass students are more accepting of anal sex. Overall, only 32% of first-year students think it's totally fine, whereas 41% of seniors do.

## Results over 30 years:

Over the past 30 years, **Anal sex has become more acceptable, especially to men.** While only half of college men felt anal sex was totally acceptable in the early 1990s, today over three-quarters of men feel this way.

# What's love got to do with it?

**College students were asked, "How important is it for you to be in love with the person you are having sex with?"**

Response options ranged from "very important" to "unimportant."

**For most people, love and sex are closely linked. That is, unless you're a college student.**

Just over half (56%) of college students say being in love is important. The term "making love" is less likely to be used by today's college students to describe this activity.

## College students responded:

**56% say being in love is important**

**Love might be endangered, but it is not extinct!**

The differences in responses by college women and men reveal that when it comes to some things with sex, the double standard is alive and well. Many more college women (62%) feel love is important in a sexual relationship, whereas far fewer college men (42%) feel the same way. Conversely, a quarter of college men (27%) say being in love is <u>not</u> important when it comes to sex (and perhaps not even knowing his partner's name?), whereas only 14% of women say this. For many college students today (men especially), sex is not seen as something special you do with someone special.

## Results over 30 years:

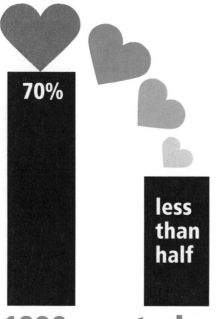

70%

less than half

1990s **vs.** today

In the past 30 years, being in love as an important component of sex has fallen sharply from about 70% in the early 1990s to now less than half of college students seeing love as important. Over time, love has taken a backseat in the sexual relationships of college students. Sex has become detached from love.

**Being in love as an important component of sex has fallen sharply**

# How comfortable are you having a gay friend?

**College students were asked about their level of comfort with having a gay friend.** They were asked to consider a situation in which they discover their best friend is gay when she/he reveals the desire to have a sexual experience. Response options to measure level of comfort ranged from unaccepting (*"One of distress. I would terminate the relationship,"* and *"I would refuse the invite and say that our friendship depends on the homosexuality being kept private,"*) to accepting (*"I would refuse the invitation, but say that their homosexuality would not affect our friendship,"* and *"I would be pleased."*)

# 85% are accepting of their gay friends

For the 5,237 students who consider themselves exclusively heterosexual, most (85%) indicate they were accepting of their gay friend and this would not affect their relationship.

**Many more women (91%) than men (71%) indicate their acceptance** and that this would not affect their relationship. In contrast, one out of five (19%) of the college men say they would want to terminate the relationship, while few (6%) of the women would do so.

**Results over 30 years:**

**Looking across the 30 years,** there has been a dramatic increase in the proportion of students who report that they are accepting of a gay friend, **increasing from 60% in the early 1990s to more than 90% today.**

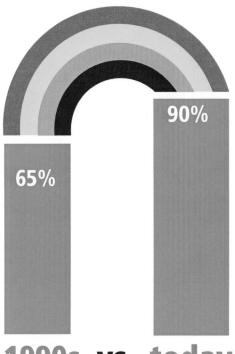

65%

90%

dramatic increase in the proportion of students who report that they are accepting of a gay friend

1990s vs. today

# What are your feelings about abortion?

**College men and women were asked about their feelings on abortion.** Specifically, students were asked how supportive they are of the Supreme Court decision, *Roe v Wade*, which legalized abortion. Responses ranged from "I fully agree" to "I fully disagree."

# 77% agree with the *Roe v Wade* decision

The majority (77%) of students agree with the Supreme Court decision on abortion. Some (20%) are opposed to abortion, but feel there should be exceptions made for the health of the mother and in cases of rape. Few (3%) disagree and feel it should be overturned.

In addition, the longer you are in college, the more supportive you become. While 74% of first-year students fully support *Roe v Wade,* 82% of seniors fully support this Supreme Court decision.

## Results over 30 years:

**Across the past three decades, most college students continue to fully support a woman's right to choose.**

However, there was a decline in full support of *Roe v Wade* in the past 30 years, as an increasing number of students said it should be allowed only in certain circumstances, such as when a mother's life is in danger or in the case of rape. Full support of *Roe v Wade* went from a high of 85% in the early 1990s to 70% in the early 2000s. However, since that time, there has been an increase, with most college students today saying they fully support *Roe v Wade* — the same percentage as in the early 1990s (85%).

There has been strong support of *Roe v Wade* across the 30 years.

# Parental Influence:

## 1990–2020 Data

1. What would mom say if she knew?

2. What would dad say if he knew?

3. Ever asked mom a question about sex?

4. Ever asked dad a question about sex?

5. Did your parents influence your views on sex?

# What would mom say if she knew?

**College students were asked, "What is your mother's feelings about your having premarital sex?"** Options were "She would be opposed," "She would not mind if we were in love" or "She would be in favor of it." Students were also given the option "I don't know."

## 74% think mom would say:

**OK if in love 54%**

**Opposed 23%**

**In favor 23%**

**26% don't know what mom would say.**

One-quarter (26%) of students say they don't know what mom's feelings are. Of the 74% who expressed an opinion, more than half (54%) feel she would not mind if they were in love. For mom, love should have something to do with it. However, about a quarter (23%) think she would be opposed and another quarter (23%) believe their mother would be in favor.

College women are more likely than college men to think their mothers would be okay as long as they are in love (56% vs. 48%). On the other hand, many more college men than women feel their mothers would be in favor of them having premarital sex (31% of the men vs. only 21% of the women).

## Results over 30 years:

**Across 30 years,** there has been an increase in college students believing that their mom would not only be okay but be in favor of them having sex (from 15% to nearly 40% today). Conversely, there has been a decrease in the proportion of college students believing that their mom would be opposed (from 30% to 10% today).

# 1990s vs. today
**More students today think mom would either be OK with premarital sex if they were in love, or in favor of them having sex.**

# What would dad say if he knew?

**College students were asked, "What is your father's feelings about your having premarital sex?"** Options were "He would be opposed," "He would not mind if we were in love" or "He would be in favor of it." Students were also given the option, "I don't know."

## 59% think dad would say:

**OK if in love 40%**

**Opposed 35%**

**In favor 25%**

**41% don't know what dad would say.**

Many college students (41%) did not know their father's opinion. Of the 59% who had an opinion about their dad's perspective, 35% say dad would be opposed, and nearly as many (40%) feel he would be okay if love was involved. Fewer (25%) believe he would be in favor.

Remnants of the double standard are reflected in the student responses about their dad. **College women are much more likely than college men to report their father is opposed to her having premarital sex (44% vs. 16%).** In contrast, men are much more likely than women (49% vs. 13%) to report their father is in favor of him having premarital sex. Women are more likely than men to report their father would not mind if they were in love (43% and 35%).

## Results over 30 years:

**Across time, there has been an increase in students who think their father is in favor (from 20% to nearly 35% today).** This increase is due primarily to the many men who feel their father is in favor (from 40% in the early 1990s to over 60% today). College women (more than men) report that their father would be opposed or would not mind as long as they were in love.

60%

40%

# 1990s vs. today

**40% to 60% today of college men think dad is in favor!**

# Ever asked mom a question about sex?

**College students were asked, "How often did you ask your mother questions about sexuality before you came to college?"** Response options ranged from "Never" to "Very frequently."

## A little over half have asked mom a question or two

**36%**
never asked mom a sex question

About one-third (36%) of college students report they have never asked their mother a question related to sex. A little over half (53%) have at least asked a question or two. Few (11%) indicated that they have often or frequently asked their mom questions about sex.

**53%**
asked mom one or two questions

College women (69%) are much more likely than college men (53%) to report they have asked their mother a question.

**11%**
asked mom frequent sex questions

What is masturbation?

**Results over 30 years:**

MOM

**Despite years of advocating the importance of parents as sexual educators of their children,**
**there has been very little change.**

Across the 30 years, the proportion of students who report they have asked their mother questions about sex has remained static.

What is an orgasm?

# Ever asked dad a question about sex?

**College students were asked, "How often did you ask your father questions about sexuality before you came to college?** Response options ranged from "Never" to "Very frequently."

## Dad is nearly nonexistent in conversations about sex.

**75%**
never asked dad
a sex question

Dad is nearly nonexistent in the conversations about sex. The majority (75%) of college students report they have <u>never</u> asked their father a single question about sex. However, almost a quarter (22%), say they have at least approached dad with a question about sex once or twice. Barely 3% say they often turn to dad for answers to sex questions.

**22%**
asked dad
one or two
questions

**3%**
asked dad
frequent sex
questions

# What's a blow job?

## Do I need contraception?

For those few students (25%) who report they have asked their father a question, men (43%) are much more likely than women (18%) to report they have done so.

## Results over 30 years:

**Across the three decades, there has been very little change in the proportion of students who say they have asked their father questions about sex.** Most college students do not turn to their father for answers about sex-related issues.

# Did your parents influence your views on sex?

**College students were asked, "Which has been your most important source of influence on your sexuality?"** Options: mother, father, both parents equally, siblings of the same sex, siblings of the other sex, friends of the same sex, friends of the other sex, religion, media or school.

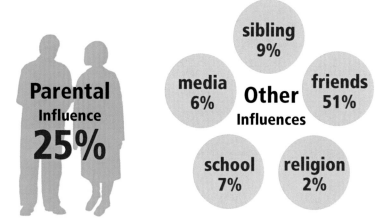

Only one-quarter (25%) report that their parents (mother, father or both parents equally) are the most important source of influence on their sexuality. The majority of students say their friends (51%) are the most important influence on their sexual attitudes, particularly same-sex friends (41%).

Other influences identified less frequently as an influence were siblings (9%), school (7%), media (6%) and religion (2%)

## Results over 30 years:

Across the years, friends are identified as the most important influence on college students' sexual attitudes, especially same-sex friends.

Friends have the most influence on sexual attitudes.

Across the three decades, there was **a decrease in the role of friends (from 60% to 45% today). They have been replaced in the last decade by the media** as an increasing source of influence (from 5% to 20% today).

**For most students, parents are not seen as a big influence on their sex lives.**

# Safer Sex
# and HIV/AIDS:

## 1990–2020
## Data

1. How concerned are you about HIV/AIDS?

2. Has your behavior changed in response to HIV/AIDS?

**How likely are you to…..**

- Ask how many sex partners the person has had?
- Try to guess if a partner might be HIV+?
- Take fewer precautions if a partner does not seem like type?
- Ask for a monogamous relationship?
- Ask a partner if she/he has been tested for HIV?
- Have both of you tested for HIV?
- Discuss using a condom before sex?
- Refuse sex without a condom?

# How concerned are you about HIV?

**College men and women were asked, "How concerned are you that HIV/AIDS will spread widely among the nation's college students/young adults?"** Response options: very concerned, somewhat concerned, not at all concerned, uncertain

The overwhelming majority of college students (88%) express concern about HIV/AIDS. Specifically, 48% are very concerned and 40% somewhat concerned.

College women are more likely than men to report they are "very concerned" (50% vs. 42%) that HIV will spread.

## Results over 30 years:

**However, over the past three decades, the level of concern surrounding HIV/AIDS has decreased dramatically.** Fewer students are "very concerned" today compared to 30 years ago. The further we have moved from the time when HIV first became an issue in the 1980s and was seen by many as a death sentence, the less concern there is. This change is seen in the 1990s, perhaps with the introduction of better treatment that changed the face of AIDS to a long-term, manageable illness. While more than three-quarters of college students were very concerned in the 1990s, less than one-quarter (20%) of students today indicate they are very concerned. In addition, very few (less than 1%) were unconcerned in the 1990s, whereas today almost 20% of college students say they are not concerned at all about HIV/AIDS.

**Over 30 years,** the level of concern surrounding HIV/AIDS has **decreased dramatically.**

# Has your behavior changed in response to HIV?

**College students were asked, "Has your behavior changed in response to the HIV/AIDS epidemic?" and given the response options of either Yes or No.**

## Both men and women responded

# No.

Two-thirds of college students (65%) report they have not changed their behavior in response to HIV/AIDS.

There was no difference in the proportion of college men and women who report they changed their behavior in response to the HIV/AIDS epidemic.

In terms of class standing, the longer they are in college, the more likely they are to say they have changed their behavior in response to HIV.

| 30% | 32% | 38% | 44% |
| first-year | sophomores | juniors | seniors |

**Results over 30 years:**

**In the past 30 years, there has been a**
## significant decrease
**in the proportion of students who report that they have changed their behavior, from 60% of students in the 1990s to 30% today.** For many of today's college students, the AIDS epidemic is perceived as a distant memory and therefore a decreasing number of college students don't see an urgency to change their behavior. For others, HIV has been a reality for their generation, resulting in safer sex practices. They are not changing their behavior because they are already practicing safer sex.

# I changed my behavior

60%   30%
## 1990s **vs.** today

# How likely are you to... ask how many sex partners the person has had?

**A majority (78%) of students indicate they were likely to ask a potential sex partner how many partners he or she has had.**

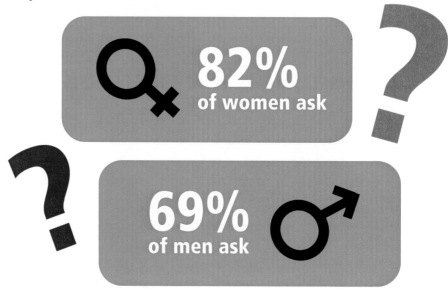

Women were more likely than men (82% of women vs. 69% of men) to say they would ask a potential partner about the number of previous partners.

## Results over 30 years:

Despite an increase in the late 1990s and early 2000s in the number of college students who said they would ask about previous sex partners (80% would ask), college students today are less likely to ask how many previous sex partners a person has had (60% today).

## College students today are
# less likely
## to ask how many previous partners...

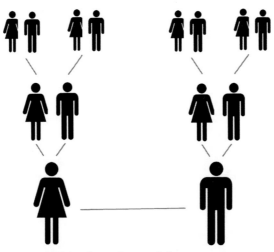

...you're sleeping with everyone
your partner has slept with :(

# How likely are you to... try to guess if a partner might be HIV+?

**More than half (56%) of students indicate they are likely to guess if their partner might be HIV+.** And men and women are equally likely to try to guess if their potential partner is HIV+.

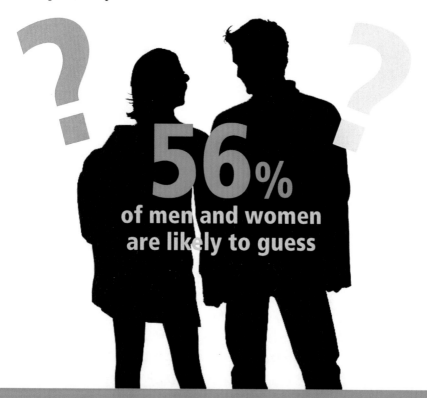

**56%** of men and women are likely to guess

**Results over 30 years:**

As we look over time, today's college students are much less likely to try to guess if their partner might be HIV+ as compared to those in the early 1990s, from 70% back then to 45% today.

likely to guess HIV+

70%    45%

1990s vs. today

# How likely are you to... take fewer precautions if a partner does not seem like the type?

**Less than half (45%) of college students say they'd take fewer precautions if a partner does not seem like the type to be infected.**

Men were more likely than women to say they would take fewer precautions if their potential sex partner does not seem like the type to be infected. Men were more likely than women to be risk takers and forgo such things as using a condom if the person does not seem like the type. (52% of men vs. only 42% of women.)

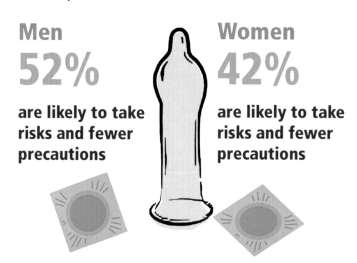

**Men**

## 52%

are likely to take risks and fewer precautions

**Women**

## 42%

are likely to take risks and fewer precautions

## Results over 30 years:

**From the early 1990s to 2000, the percentage of students who say they are likely to take**

## fewer precautions dropped from 60% to about 30%.

However, since 2000, there has been an increase in risk-taking, with nearly half of college students saying they are likely to take fewer precautions if a potential sex partner does not seem like the type to be infected.

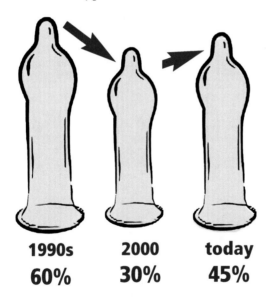

| 1990s | 2000 | today |
|-------|------|-------|
| **60%** | **30%** | **45%** |

## likely to take fewer precautions

# How likely are you to... ask for a monogamous relationship?

**Three-quarters (73%) of students indicated they are likely to ask to have a monogamous relationship.** Women are more likely than men to say they are likely to ask to have a monogamous relationship (78% of women vs. 63% of men).

ask to be
## Monogamous
# 73%

**Women**

# 78%
**ask for a monogamous relationship**

**Men**

# 63%
**ask for a monogamous relationship**

**Results over 30 years:**

**When examining trends over 30 years, there was an**

## increase from the early 1990s to 2000

**in college students' likelihood of asking their partner for a monogamous relationship (from about 75% to 85%).** However, in the past 20 years, fewer students say they are likely to do this — only about 60%

## I want to be the only one!

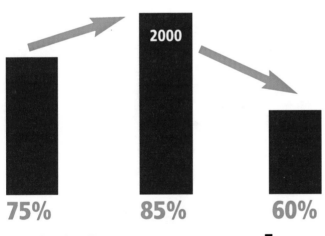

**1990s** vs. **today**

# How likely are you to... ask a partner if she/he has been tested for HIV?

**Half (50%) of college students say they are likely to ask their potential sex partners if they have been tested.**

Women are more likely than men to say they will ask their sex partners if they have been tested (54% vs. 39%)

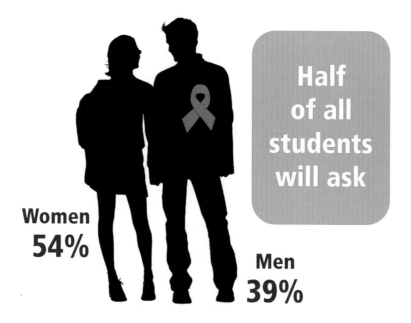

**Half of all students will ask**

**Women 54%**

**Men 39%**

**Results over 30 years:**

## Over time, attitudes toward testing have changed greatly.

In the early 1990s only 20% of college students were likely to ask their partner about being tested, but by the late 1990s, 60% were likely to do this. However, since 2000, less than half of college students say they are likely to inquire about if their partner has had an HIV antibody test.

2000

20%  60%  45%

## 1990s vs. today

# How likely are you to... have both of you tested for HIV?

**A minority of college students (36%) indicated they are likely to have both of them tested for HIV antibodies.**

College women were much more likely than college men to say they would have both of them tested for HIV antibodies (39% of women and 29% of men).

# 36% are likely to have both of them tested.

**39%**
of women

**29%**
of men

## Results over 30 years:

### In terms of change over time,

**the first half of the 1990s saw
an increase in the likelihood of having both
people tested (from 11% to 50% by 1995).**

**However, after 1995, this likelihood declined.**

Fewer college students say they would insist that both they
and their partner be tested. Since 1996, only about a third
(36%) say they are likely to have both of them be tested for
HIV antibodies.

11%          50%          36%

## 1990s vs. today

# How likely are you to... discuss using a condom before sex?

**A majority (90%) of students indicate they are likely to discuss using a condom before having sex.**

Women are more likely than men to say they will discuss using a condom with a potential partner (91% of women vs. 85% of men).

**Discuss use of condoms**

# 90%
### are likely to discuss using a condom

**Results over 30 years:**

Although the likelihood of discussing condom use with a partner has remained high across the 30 years (90% or higher), there has been a slow, gradual decline in more recent years.

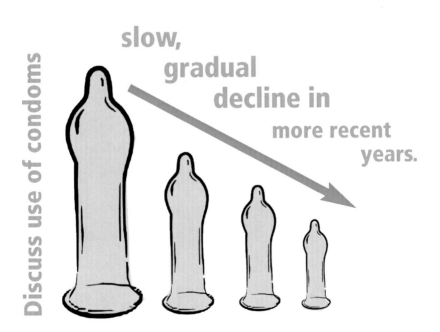

slow, gradual decline in more recent years.

Discuss use of condoms

# How likely are you to... refuse sex without a condom?

**Three-quarters (75%) of students indicated they are likely to refuse sexual activity without a condom.**

Women are more likely than men to say they will refuse sex without a condom (82% vs. 59%).

**75% No condom, no sex.**

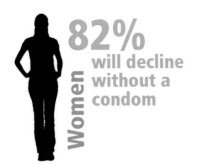

82% will decline without a condom

Women

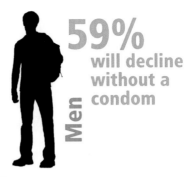

59% will decline without a condom

Men

## Results over 30 years:

**Looking across the past three decades, there was an increase in the number of students who said they would refuse sex without a condom in the early 1990s.** This increase remained high through 2005. **However, since that time, there has been a decline, with fewer college students today saying they would be likely to refuse sex without a condom —— the same as in the early 1990s (65%).**

2005

65%    85%    65%

1990s vs. today

# Difficult Side of Sexuality:

## 1990–2020 Data

1. Do you know anyone who has had an STI?

2. Ever had an STI?

3. Know anyone who has had an abortion?

4. Ever been involved in a pregnancy that ended in abortion?

5. Do you know anyone who has been raped?

6. Have you ever been raped?

7. Ever had an involuntary sexual experience?

8. Were you sexually abused as a child?

# Do you know anyone who has had an STI?

**College students were asked, Do you know anyone personally who has had a sexually transmitted infection?**

## YES
## 56%

**Most college students (56%) say they know someone who has had a sexually transmitted infection (STI).** This should come as no surprise, since STIs and college students remain an ongoing concern.

**There is no difference between college women and men who know someone with an STI** (56% and 55%).

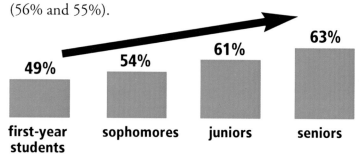

| 49% | 54% | 61% | 63% |
|-----|-----|-----|-----|
| first-year students | sophomores | juniors | seniors |

The longer they are in college, the more likely they are to say they personally know someone who has had a sexually transmitted infection.

**Results over 30 years:**

Across time, the proportion of college students who say they know someone who has had a STI has decreased — from 65% in the early 1990s to 55% today. However, in the past few years there has been an uptick.

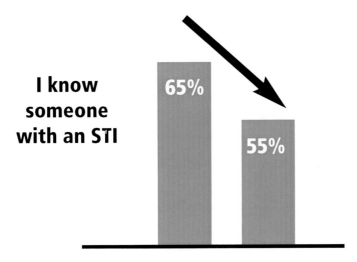

I know someone with an STI

65%

55%

**1990s vs. today**

# Ever had an STI?

**College students were asked, "Have you ever had a sexually transmitted infection (STI)?"**

Eight percent of sexually active college men and women say they have had a sexually transmitted infection.

## women        men

8%        8%

There was no difference between college men and women.

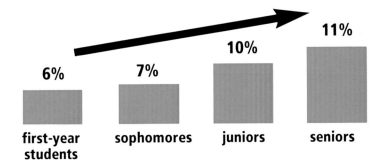

6%      7%      10%      11%

first-year students    sophomores    juniors    seniors

In terms of class standing, the longer students have been in college, the more likely they are to say that they have had an STI — from 6% of first-year students to 11% of seniors saying they have had an STI.

## Results over 30 years:

**Across time, the proportion of college students who report having an STI has decreased,** from a high of 15% in the early 1990s to a low of 6% today, reflecting greater safer sex practices by these students in recent years.

# Know anyone who has had an abortion?

**College students were asked, "Do you know anyone personally who has had an abortion?"**

## 59%
**know someone who has.**

Over half of college student (59%) reported that they knew someone who has had an abortion.

**Women (63%) were much more likely than men (50%)** to know someone personally who has had an abortion.

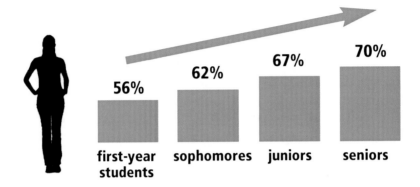

The longer students have been in college, the more likely they are to say that they know someone personally who has had an abortion. For women especially, there was an increase from 56% of first year women to 70% of senior women knowing someone who had an abortion.

## Results over 30 years:

**75%**

**With fewer unplanned pregnancies across the past three decades, the proportion of** **40%** **students who reported they know someone personally who has had an abortion has also decreased — from 75% in the early 1990s to 40% today.**

# Ever been involved in a pregnancy that ended in abortion?

College students were asked, "Have you been involved in a pregnancy that ended in abortion?"

**4%**
of college students have.

Few (4%) college students report that they had been involved in a pregnancy that ended in abortion.

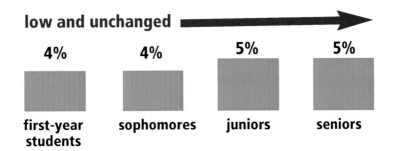

**low and unchanged** ⟶

| **4%** | **4%** | **5%** | **5%** |
| first-year students | sophomores | juniors | seniors |

There is no difference between college women and men who had experienced this and no difference by class standing.

## Results over 30 years:

**Across time, the proportion of college students who report they been involved with a pregnancy that ended in an abortion remained low and actually decreased over the 30 years.**

# Do you know anyone who has been raped?

**College students were asked, "Do you know anyone personally who has been raped?"**

# 53%
**of college students know some- one who has.**

Slightly more than half of college students (53%) know someone personally who has been raped. Women are more likely than men to know someone (54% vs. 48%)

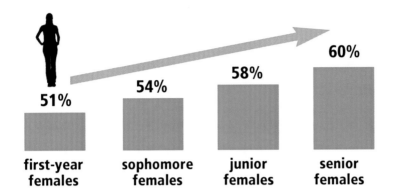

51% first-year females

54% sophomore females

58% junior females

60% senior females

The proportion of college women who report they know someone personally who had been raped increased the longer they had been in college, from half (51%) of first-year women to 60% of senior women knowing someone who had been raped.

## Results over 30 years:

**Over the past 30 years, the proportion of college students who reported they know someone personally who had been raped had remained relatively unchanged.** In the last five years there has been an increase in the number of students who know someone (from just over half to 65% today). **This may be related to the #MeToo movement, and greater discussion and awareness of sexual assault issues.**

# Have you ever been raped?

**College students were asked, "Have you ever been raped?"**

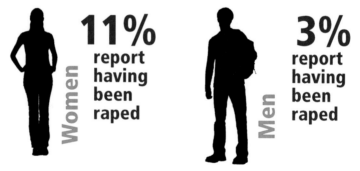

**9%** of college students report that they have experienced rape.

**11%** report having been raped

Women

**3%** report having been raped

Men

College women are more likely to say they have been raped as compared to men (11% vs. 3%)

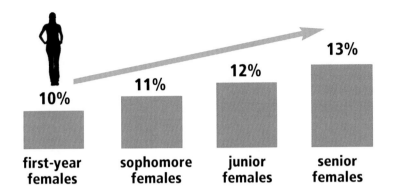

10%
first-year
females

11%
sophomore
females

12%
junior
females

13%
senior
females

In terms of class standing, the proportion of women who report they had been raped increased the longer they had been in college, from 10% of first-year women to 13% of seniors. **That is one in eight college women.**

## Results over 30 years:

Across the past 30 years, the proportion of college students who report that they have been raped remained relatively unchanged. However, in the last five years, the proportion of women who say they have been raped has increased (from about 10% to 15% today).

# Ever had an involuntary sexual experience?

**College students were asked, "Have you ever been involved in an involuntary sexual experience?"**

**31%**

One-third (31%) of college students report having been involved in an involuntary sexual experience.

**Women**

**37%**
had an involuntary sexual experience

**Men**

**15%**
had an involuntary sexual experience

College women (37%) are much more likely than college men (15%) to report that they have been involved in an involuntary sexual experience.

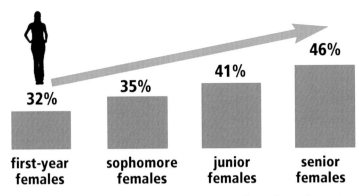

**32%** first-year females

**35%** sophomore females

**41%** junior females

**46%** senior females

In terms of class standing, the longer students have been in college, the more likely they are to say that they have been involved in an involuntary sexual experience. It is women who are more likely to say they experienced involuntary sexual experience - increasing from a third (32%) of first-year college women to nearly half (46%) of seniors.

## Results over 30 years:

35%

**Across the past 30 years, the proportion of students who reported they have been involved**

25%

**in an involuntary sexual experience decreased.**
However, in the last few years there has been a slight increase in women reporting that they have been involved in an involuntary sexual experience.

*Notice the discrepancy between those who said they have been raped (9%) and those who said they had experienced an involuntary sexual experience (31%). Although involuntary sexual experience refers to a broader range of behaviors, I have found that students do not usually characterize their involuntary sexual experience as rape for a number of reasons: they don't understand the definition of rape or have a sensationalized image of what "real rape" is, they don't want to categorize the person who assaulted them as a rapist, or because they blame themselves for what happened.*

# Were you sexually abused as a child?

**College students were asked, "Would you consider yourself a victim of child sexual abuse?"**

## 1:12
### were abused as children

One in 12 (8%) college students consider themselves a victim of child sexual abuse.

College women (10%) are much more likely than college men (4%) to report that they experienced childhood sexual abuse.

**Women**
**10%**

**Men**
**4%**

## Results over 30 years:

**Across the past 30 years, the proportion of college students who self-identified as victims of childhood sexual abuse decreased — from 10% in the early 1990s to 7% today.** This is consistent with declines reported in national studies, suggesting that decades of coordinated efforts to increase awareness and prevention, along with better training of professionals and the prosecution of offenders, have brought down the rate of child sexual abuse.

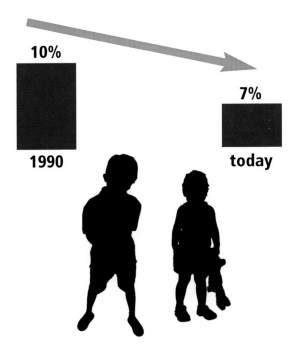

10%

1990

7%

today

# Newer Data Set

## 2010–2020*

1. Have you used the morning-after pill?
2. Do you do a monthly self-exam?
3. Penis size? Breast size?
4. Have you ever shaved?
5. Sex without a condom?
6. What have you done sexually?
7. Technology and sex
8. Planes, trains and automobiles
9. Ever lied to get someone in bed?
10. Ever gotten someone drunk?
11. Had an intentional one-night stand?
12. Ever cheated on a partner?
13. Why are you most likely to have sex?
14. How does your sex life stack up?
15. Longest you've gone without sex?
16. Greatest age difference?
17. The adjective that best describes sex?
18. Favorite position?
19. How often do you reach orgasm?
20. Are you satisfied?

*Results are based on responses of 2,416 students

# Have you used the morning-after pill?

**College men and women were asked, "Have you ever used emergency contraception?"**

**For those students who reported they were sexually active, a third of respondents report they used emergency contraception, the pill taken soon after unprotected sex to prevent pregnancy.**

## 1/3
### have used the morning-after pill

Many more college women than men reported that emergency contraception was used (37% vs. 22%). Perhaps one reason for the discrepancy — he did not know she had taken it. The proportion of college students who report using emergency contraception has remained the same across 10 years.

# Do you do a monthly self-exam?

**College students were asked about self-exams. Women were asked, "Do you do a regular/monthly breast self-exam? Men were asked "Do you do a regular/ monthly testicular self-exam?"**

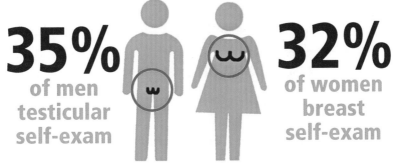

**35%**
of men
testicular
self-exam

**32%**
of women
breast
self-exam

Although the American Cancer Society recommends a monthly self-exam for early detection of breast and testicular cancers, the survey found only about a third of college students say they do this.

Only 35% of men and 32% of women report that they do self-exams. Although there was a slight upward trend across the decade, **clearly there is more work to do on the prevention front.**

# Penis size?
# Breast Size?

College students were asked to rate themselves. For men: "How do you rate the size of your penis?" For women: "How do you rate the size of your breasts?" The response options: "Below average," "About Average," and "Above Average."

## Half the students rated their body parts as "about average."

It should come as no surprise that there were big differences between men and women when it comes to "below average," with many more women rating their breasts this way (26%), while few men rated their penis size as below average (8%). College men do not seem to have the insecurities of penis size. Across the decade, greater numbers of women rated their breasts as "below average."

**8%** rate their penis size below average

**Men**

**26%** rate their breast size below average

**Women**

# Have you ever shaved?

**College students were asked, "Have you ever shaved your pubic area?" Response options ranged from "trim," "partial," "full," "all of the above" or "never."**

**98% yes**

**Nearly every student surveyed says he or she shaves — a full 98%.**

College men are just as likely as women to say they shave their pubic region, but there appears to be variations in how much hair they remove. More women say they remove all their pubic hair as compared to men (46% vs. 21%). On the other hand, men are more likely than women to say they only trim or partially shave (26% vs. 10%). Across the decade there was an increase in men reporting they remove all their pubic hair (from 15% to 30% today).

Pubic hair removal is the new norm among today's college men and women. Whether it is due to the rise in skimpy bathing suits, oral sex or porn stars shaving in order to increase and enhance the view of their genitals, pubic hair shaving has become mainstream.

# Sex without a condom?

**College students were asked, "Since coming to college, have you had sex without a condom because…." and a range of reasons were given.**

|  | Women | Men |
|---|---|---|
| I was sure that my partner was disease free. | 50% | 45% |
| I just assumed my partner was disease free. | 31% | 33% |
| I was drunk or high. | 32% | 30% |
| I didn't care. | 25% | 30% |
| I didn't want to spoil the mood. | 21% | 21% |
| I was lazy. | 15% | 20% |

|                                          | Women | Men |
|------------------------------------------|-------|-----|
| My partner was too hot.                  | 11%   | 20% |
| I was worried about my partner's response. | 10% | 7% |
| My partner refused to use a condom.      | 7%    | 9%  |

For many of these reasons, college men and women are similar. These findings were consistent across the decade.

However, **more men than women** say they don't use a condom because: **they don't care, they are lazy or think their partner is too hot.**

She was too hot to stop!!!

:-)

# What have you done sexually?

## College students were asked to check what they have done sexually from a list of options.

When looking at the responses for those who are sexually active, we see that college students engage in a variety of sexual behaviors.

| | Women | Men |
|---|---|---|
| **Talked dirty** | 88% | 89% |
| **Included spanking** | 70% | 72% |
| **Used a vibrator or other sex toy by yourself*** | 50% | 14% |
| **Included a vibrator or other sex toy with a partner** | 30% | 27% |
| **Included role play in your sexual experience** | 26% | 29% |
| **Included bondage (e.g. you or your partner tied up)** | 33% | 39% |

*includes those who said they have masturbated

Across the past 10 years, there has been an increase in the proportion of college students who report engaging in these behaviors.

|  | Women | Men |
|---|---|---|
| **Had a "friend with benefits"** | 65% | 68% |
| **Had a one night stand** | 53% | 64% |
| **Made out with someone of the same sex just because**\*\* | 41% | 5% |
| **Had a threesome** | 11% | 15% |
| **Had sex with a much older person** | 15% | 15% |

You did *what*?

\*\* includes those who indicated they are a 0 or 1 on the Kinsey Scale.

# Technology and sex

**College students were asked, "In terms of use of technology, have you ever…" and were instructed to check off whatever they have participated in.**

## The Internet, social media and cell phones have given us more options than ever before when it comes to sex.

According to these results, sexting (the sending or receiving of nude pictures) is fairly common, as is being photographed nude. Phone sex is still around and now is complimented by the increasing popularity of sex online. All of these activities have increased over the decade.

Nearly all the college men say and two-thirds of the college women say they have viewed pornography online. In addition, two-thirds of college students say they have watched an X-rated movie. The proportion of college students reporting they view pornography and watch X-rated movies has remained the same across the decade.

| | Women | Men |
|---|---|---|
| Received nude pictures of someone else? | 71% | 79% |
| Had nude pictures taken of yourself? | 53% | 45% |
| Sent nude pictures of yourself to someone? | 65% | 51% |
| Been filmed having sex?* | 18% | 21% |
| Had phone sex?* | 34% | 39% |
| Had sex online?• | 16% | 21% |
| Met someone online for sex?* | 11% | 18% |
| Viewed pornography online (pictures or video) | 71% | 95% |
| Watched an X-rated movie | 54% | 78% |

*includes only those students who said they have had sex

# Planes, trains and automobiles

College students were asked, "Where have you had sex?" and were presented with a checklist of places.

## Places:

**Have you ever had sex:**

| | Total |
|---|---|
| outdoors? | 60% |
| in a public building? | 29% |
| in your parent's bed? | 25% |
| at your workplace? | 11% |
| in the library? | 4% |
| in a nightclub/bar? | 4% |

**College students report that sex isn't just for the bedroom.** Both college men and women report similar experiences in the various venues, with very little change across the decade. The most common is in a car (75%), followed by outdoors (60%). Only 2% have membership in the mile high club. A third have taken a chance by having sex in a public building, and about a quarter have had sex in their parents' bed. And as these results show, there is more going on in the library stacks than studying for 4% of college students.

## Transportation:

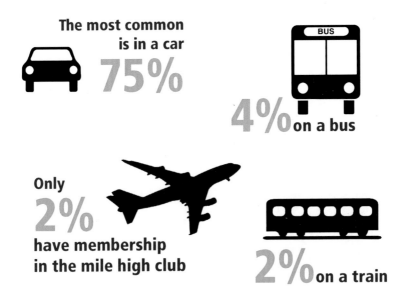

The most common is in a car

**75%**

**4%** on a bus

Only **2%** have membership in the mile high club

**2%** on a train

# Ever lied to get someone in bed?

**Students were asked, "Have you ever lied to get someone in bed?"** Approximately 1 in 12 college students (8%) say they have lied in order to get someone to have sex. This has remained about the same across the decade.

## 1 in 5 men

## 8% HAVE LIED
### to get someone to have sex

### only 1:20 women

When we compare college men and women, **it was mostly the men— nearly one in five (19%)** who say they have done this.

Just a heads up about the pickup lines.

# Ever gotten someone drunk?

**College men and women were asked, "Have you ever tried to get someone drunk or high in order to get that person into bed?"** Few college students (5%) say they have tried to get someone drunk or high in order to get that person into bed. The percent of college students who say they have done this has gone down over the past 10 years.

When comparing men and women, **college men were much more likely than college women** to say they have done this (10% vs. only 4%)

**Few college students say they've done this**

# Had an intentional one-night stand?

**College students were asked, "Have you ever slept with someone knowing you would never call again?"**

Approximately a third of students (32%) report sleeping with someone knowing they would never call him or her again. This percentage has gone up over the decade — from 29% to 35% today.

Many more college men (44%) than college women (28%) say they have done this.

## knowing they would never call him or her again

| Women | Men |
|-------|-----|
| **28%** vs. | **44%** |

# Ever cheated on a partner?

**College students were asked, "Have you ever cheated on a steady partner?"**

Approximately one in five college students (22%) say they have cheated on a steady partner. There is little difference between college men and women who say they have done this (22% of women vs. 24% of men). Fewer students today say they have cheated on a steady partner as compared to a decade ago.

# 1:5
## have cheated

## little difference
## in men and women

# Why are you most likely to have sex?

**College men and women were asked, "The reason you are <u>most likely</u> to have sex with someone is...."**

The top two responses were **love 48% and attraction 44%**

**XOX**

Across the decade, love declined and attraction increased as the most likely reason to have sex with someone.

College men say the reason they are most likely to have sex is because the person is attractive (65%), while women said they do it for love (55%).

**The double standard endures the test of time.**

| Women | Men |
|---|---|
| **55% say love** | **65% say attractive** |

# How does your sex life stack up?

**College students were asked, "Compared to other people your age, your sex life is…" with response options of better than most, about the same or not as good.**

Less than half (42%) of college students feel their sex life is about the same as their peers. About one-third (31%) feel that their sex life is better than most and another one-third (28%) feel their sex life is not as good as others.

**There are no differences between men and women, or responses across the decade.**

**42%** about the same
**31%** better
**28%** not as good

# Longest you've gone without sex?

**College students were asked, "Since coming to college, what is the longest you have gone without having sex?" Response options ranged from a few days, weeks, months or a year or more.**

## 50%
### have gone
### a few months
### or more
### without sex

Despite an image of college involving sex every weekend, half (50%) of the sexually active college students say they have gone a few months or more without sex (8% of these have gone a year or more). More than a third (37%) have gone a few weeks. The rest of the college students (13%) report they have gone a few days without sex. There is little difference between college men and women on this question, and their responses across the decade.

# Greatest age difference?

## Similar age
## 80%

**College students were asked, "What has been the greatest age difference between you and a consensual sex partner?"**

Most say their sex partners are similar in age (80%). This has remained consistent across the  decade. College women are more likely to say they have had an older partner, with nearly 20% having had a sex partner five or more years their senior. When it comes to the "cougar effect," 5% of the college men say they have had a sexual partner who is 10 or more years older.

# The adjective that best describes sex?

**College students were asked, "What adjective best describes your attitude toward sex?"**

Most college students describe their attitude toward sex as:
**adventurous 35%, self-confident 26% cautious 20%**

Few chose adjectives such as "kinky," "confused," or "uncomfortable" to describe their attitude toward sex.

In terms of differences between college men and women in the way they describe their attitudes toward sex, college men are more likely to say they are adventurous (42%) while college women are more likely than men to say they are cautious (23%). In an interesting twist, the proportion of students who chose "self-confident" decreased, while the proportion who chose "kinky" to describe their attitude toward sex increased across the decade.

**Women 23%**
say they are
**cautious**

**Men 42%**
say they are
**adventurous**

# Favorite Position?

**College students were asked, "What is your favorite sexual position?" and given response options: missionary or man on top, woman on top, doggie style, the spoon or not applicable/none of these are my favorite.**

For those who had a preference, the most popular positions are:

## woman on top
## man on top

30%

34%

## doggie style

31%

### few chose spooning 4%

In terms of differences between the genders, college men say their favorite position is doggie style (42% men vs. 27% women), whereas college women say their favorite is having the man on top (39% women vs. 20% men). Looking across the decade, doggie style increased in popularity.

men prefer doggie style

women prefer men on top

# How often do you reach orgasm?

**College students were asked, "How often do you achieve orgasm during sex with someone?"**
Responses ranged from always to never.

## **most women** do not reach orgasm through intercourse

Men **90% of men say most or all of the time**

When looking at the differences between women and men, college men are much more likely to say they reach orgasm most or all the time (88%). **On the other hand, more than half the women say they don't usually reach orgasm (59%). In fact, more than** a third of college women (41%) say they rarely or never reach orgasm with sex. The reality is many women do not reach orgasm through intercourse. Across the decade, a greater proportion of women say they rarely or never reach orgasm during sex.

# Are you satisfied?

**College students were asked, "Are you satisfied with the amount of sex you are having?"**

 **64% said yes**

Most sexually active college students say they are satisfied (64%), and this has remained relatively unchanged across the decade. However, when looking at the gender differences, college men are more likely than women to say they are not satisfied (44% of men vs. 33% of the women). Nearly half of the men are looking for more.

**However:**

 **44% of men say they are not satisfied**

 **33% of women say they are not satisfied**

# Conclusion

What these results confirm is that college is a learning experience in more ways than one. College is not just about academics. Students are on a journey to learn not only about a specific career area, but to learn more about themselves, to discover themselves. They are exposed to new ideas and a diversity of people with different values and experiences. As the survey results indicate, students become more accepting of others and the range of behaviors. And although most arrive at college having already experienced sexual intercourse, the results indicate that they are engaging in a variety of sexual activities that increase with each year they are enrolled. We have a responsibility to prepare them so that they can make informed choices.

The results suggest many positive changes have taken place in the past 30 years in such areas as use of birth control and condoms, and the resulting decline in unplanned pregnancies, abortions and STIs. Women are more in tune with their own pleasure. And we have also seen dramatic changes in attitudes, with an accelerated acceptance of such behaviors as oral and anal sex, as well as greater acceptance and understanding of sexual diversity for people who are lesbian and gay. And while love may be endangered (less than half of today's college students think it's important), it is not extinct.

On the other hand, some things have not necessarily changed at all (e.g., he says he almost always reaches orgasm with sex, while she says she usually does not), or have not changed for the better. While prior generations tended to believe sex was something you did for enjoyment with someone who was important to you or whom you at least liked, now it appears to be something you just do. Contemporary terms like "hooking up" and "friends with benefits" suggest new sexual behaviors for today's college students, but 30 years ago, it was simply called "casual sex." There has not been a rise in the percentage of college students having multiple (5 or more) partners. What has changed is that, by referring to casual sex as "friends with benefits," today's college women are able to participate in what used to be seen as a male-dominated world of casual sex. As they have learned from Facebook, a friend is no longer someone you need to know intimately.

Many of today's entering college students have not been educated in a critical area of their lives — the sexual part. What "sex education" they might have received has too often been too little, too late — and too biological. And for over three decades, our country has spent nearly $2 billion on abstinence-only-until-marriage "education" instead of focusing on providing healthy, comprehensive sexuality education. (I am for "just say no," as long as it's spelled K-N-O-W.) Along with the push for abstinence-only education came the rise in virginity pledges and virginity balls with their specific focus on girls' virginity — not boys'. It is hard to understand how we reached the point where we judge a girl's character by what is between her legs more than what is between her ears and in her heart. It is an indication the sexual double standard is still alive and well. The survey results suggest this double standard as well when we see such results across 30 years revealing:

- A college woman is more likely to say she has had fewer partners, while a man is more likely to say he has been with a higher number (slut vs. stud).
- If virginity matters, she is more likely to say she wants a partner who is experienced; he is more likely to say he wants a virgin.
- In terms of the importance of love and sex, she is more likely to say love is important; he is not. (What is important to him is if he is attracted.)
- A college woman is more likely to believe her parents would be opposed to the idea of her having sex, while a college man is more likely to think his parents (especially dad) would be in favor of it.

At the same time that these college students have been raised with the "just say no" abstinence-only message, they have been surrounded by the "just say yes" influence of living in a highly sexualized society, where exposure to adult-oriented sexually explicit material (e.g., pornography) is a mouse click away. So much of their sex education has been left to chance, uneducated peers and the Internet, resulting in many young people having unrealistic expectations of sex and arriving at college with many misconceptions. The survey findings reveal that some college students today are simply performing sex. Without the proper guidance of their parents and schools, many young people have been misled by the acting world of pornography, which is designed to be stimulating fantasy for adults. Somewhere along the line, we forgot to tell our young people that it is not intended to be sex instruction. But for too many young people, it serves as their primary foundation for sexuality education.

I see this reflected in my survey results that show that across 30 years, faking orgasm by both women and men is on the rise.

The reality versus the fantasy. Orgasm is something they have, not something they feel. At the same time there has been a rise in faking orgasm, the importance of love has dropped way off.

In addition, most young people today shave all their pubic hair, emulating what they see in porn. And a growing number of college women say they engage in same-sex eroticism for the viewing pleasure of their boyfriends. Sex now seems to be about how one appears, as many young women wonder what's wrong if they don't have simultaneous, multiple, g-spot orgasms with their "friend with benefits." At the same time, my survey has found that an increasing number of students are not concerned at all about HIV, and while most college students support abortion, there has been a growing percentage who are ambivalent about a woman's right to choose.

We are sex saturated and sex silent. We are more interested in the morality than the reality of sex. Too many people in this country think withholding information and access to services will lead to responsible behavior. As other countries have shown so clearly — Denmark, Finland, France, Germany, The Netherlands and Sweden, to name a few — this is not true and does not work. We need to begin by educating.

We teach the 3 R's (reading, writing, arithmetic) in school. I feel there should be a 4th R: relationships. For the most part, that's what sexuality education is all about. We need to help college students learn what it means to create an intimate relationship, rather than using sex as a way to avoid intimacy.

We need to help them shift from the performance model to one based in pleasure and connection. Instead of judging sex by the number of orgasms, help them judge it by how much pleasure has been created. Instead of asking, "How am I doing?" we need to help college students ask, "Am I enjoying myself?" and "Are we enjoying each other?"

---

**We teach the 3 R's (reading, writing, arithmetic) in school. I feel there should be a 4th R: relationships.**

---

How can we ever become a sexually healthy society if colleges do not educate the future teachers, doctors, lawyers, television producers and, most of all, parents? There is a real need for courses in human sexuality at all levels.

We need to focus more on real sex (the reality of what is happening in people's lives) versus reel sex (the image of what is supposedly going on via what is fed to us through the media).

This survey was designed to give us a glimpse into the lives of college students. We can begin to help by understanding their attitudes and behaviors past and present — where they have been and where they are now.

We need more honest discussions about the role of sexuality in people's lives. It is hoped that The Sex Lives of College Students can start that dialogue. We need more public discussions of private parts.

— Dr. Caron

**For more information:
thesexlivesofcollegestudents.com**